$S\sqrt{HE}$

saul williams

POCKET BOOKS

New York London Toronto Sydney

An *Original* Publication of MTV Books/Pocket Books

POCKET BOOKS, a division of Simon & Schuster Inc.
1230 Avenue of the Americas, New York, NY 10020

ISBN: 0-671-03530-4 (CD)
    0-671-03977-6

First MTV Books/Pocket Books trade paperback printing June 1999

10 9 8 7 6

POCKET and colophon are registered trademarks of Simon & Schuster Inc.

Cover Art Direction and Design by MTV Off-Air Creative
Interior Book Design by Jessica Shatan
Interior Images by Marcia Jones

Printed in the U.S.A.

For all the ghosts and corpses
that shall never know
the breath of our children

so long

for the sacrifice
and endurance
of our mothers
and the sustained breath
of our fathers

we live

For Marcia

prologue

. . . as the fearful crowd gathers
to witness my wounded sanity

slain rational
knotted tongue

calamity kisses an utterer
stuttered breath retreats
with withered desires
        ∽

most relationships are built on faults. i do not wish to place blame. but there are houses that crumble with the slightest tremble of the earth. there are those that have made homes of cliffs for centuries: families that commune with stars. we have named our daughter after one of the brightest. Saturn. yet we are left to make magic of our own names given to us through the love of our parents. she has found the ocean in her name. and i have found the sun in mine. the point where the sun is furthest from the equator: Saul Stacey = solstice. our parents were wiser than they knew.

෧෨

but this is not why i've come. i have come to tell you that i have come. on the way, i noted the women transfixed by the light coming from their centers. their heads are bowed. they have learned that if you tilt your neck to the slightest degree and hold your head just so you can look into lost worlds. they are there retrieving their young from the clutches of negligent daycare. they have come to care for the night. many of them are glowing brighter than the moon herself. thank the heavens she is not jealous in her luminescence, for i have seen many women glowing beyond the intensity of the moon and thought that perhaps the night had mirrored itself in the wake of this glorious occasion: our communion. yes, i have come. i have had a safe journey, although my fears had mounted against me. there were many mountains of my own making and valleys of days without vision.

֍

the forecast is
we kiss good-bye and never hello
all kisses are then parting kisses

and it hurts even more to write it
than it does to live it
for i know what written word can do
let alone spoken
and this is a spoken art
༄

there is a gathering in the forest. the leaves have refused to change. they say that they are tired of things never remaining the same, of dying to be reborn, of winter's dry withered hand. they are praying for an eternal spring. even i expected that the beautiful autumn must have been ecstasy for the leaves. but they admit that there is nothing more painful than changing from green to yellow to red to brown. they insist that their beauty is a prolonged suffering. they say they will never change again. they have sent me to convey their green-leafed message. winter has left them brittle and they do not wish to continue their cyclical sacrament. they wish to remain a forest, unchanging. i have told them that everything has its season. they refuse to listen and insist that i am biased because i am named after the sun's distance from the equator. they say that i am the problem. they have placed the blame on me.

∽

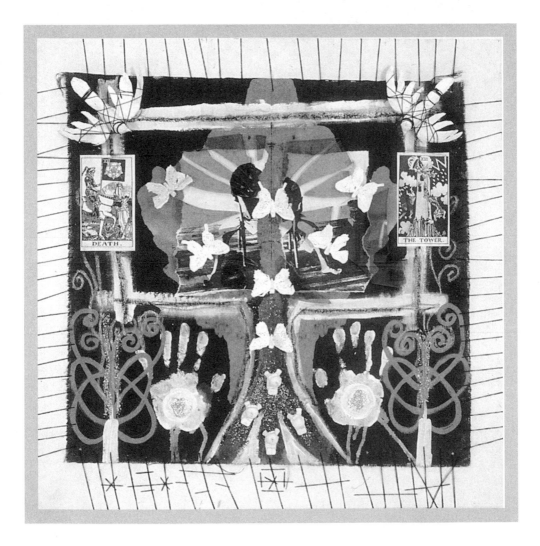

i presented
my feminine side
with flowers

she cut the stems
and placed them gently
down my throat

and these tu lips
might soon eclipse
your brightest hopes

∾

she had nothing
but time on her hands:
silver rings, turquoise stones
and purple nails

i rubbed my thumb
across her palm:
a featherbed
where slept a psalm

yea, though i walk
i used to fly
and now we dance

i watched
my toenails blacken
and walked a deadened trance

until she woke me
with the knife edge
of her glance

i have the scars to prove
the clock strikes
with her hands

             ◐

i have seen the truth
many times
but for the first time
she saw me

i wore suspenders
for the judgment
in my pants

∽

i laced my shoes with sorrow
and walked a weary road
dead end streets
don't come undone
with double knots

wing tipped shoes
that walk on air
through vacant lots

൭ഠ

she kept her deck
beneath her pillow
and had promised
me a reading

she stuck a bookmark
in my heart
and walked away

it was autumn then

the leaves
suddenly flames
the sidewalk
burning cinders

i walked the streets
as if the sun
had called me boy
mad at the world
on aging feet

shuffling
her cards

shuffling
my feet

head
to the sky
blue

the clouds
her cards

the clouds:
her cards

shuffling
the skies

a storm passes
new clouds appear:
the chariot
the priestess

the moon
in broad daylight:
an omen

෧෨

love is an unbridled horse
with one wing out-stretched
the other tucked and folded
on the right side

the horse galloping
towards a cliff
knowingly
panting just enough
for you to think
he's laughing

he?
love is male?

love is a dumb horse
with silver streaks
and a sometimes penis

a sometimes penis?

on thursdays
the rest of the week
she grazes
and paints her hooves
with red mud
making tracks

through the fields
which disappear
soon after they appear

because nature has a way
of changing
the same way
it remains

෧෨

she kept wild horses
in her stables
and rode bareback
in search of stability

i looked on
and watched
like an orphaned child
with dreams of riding
this merry go round
there are trap doors in my pockets
where lie my parents
and my admission ticket

i cannot admit
to my orphaned state
and hope to get a horse
with a saddle

i am orphaned
in her mind
and she will accept no admission
her merriness goes round
an elliptical orbit
moods gallop
toward her mechanical death

am i the suited gentleman in the carriage
the lazy eyed blacksmith
or the orphaned onlooker
who cannot afford admission
and dreams of that blue horse
striding the desolate sands
to the ocean of his fears?

he fears abandonment
and will name his children
after the return of the sun

he thought it was a distant yellow ferris wheel
that was the first time he stood without admission

his legs, scrawny tenements
ashen and bare
his eyes: broken windows
sealed with plastic
manmade and taped
to the back door
of death: his face
he had one dream

               ୧୨

she asked that i remove my dreams
before entering her home
one cannot enter a courtroom bearing arms

i had decided
to sharpen the edges
of a certain childhood fantasy
and tuck it away in my sock

emotional lavishness
can deplete memory banks
although her parents saved and saved
she knew no baptism
which is no fault
unless you have
a Christian name

i do not trust her
my plan was to attack
in the 43 seconds
that it takes eyes
to adjust to moonlight
after lights out

no one told me
that dreams glow in the dark

i was discovered
and scheduled
to be lynched
in her town square

i remind you
for every one of us you lynch
there is another burning witch

i once visited a lost world
where black men with broken necks
held the hands of charred women

they shared a love
that was as beautiful
as it was incestuous

calamity makes cousins of us all

∽

and she doesn't want to press charges
my yellow cousin
ghost of a gypsy
drunk off the wine
of pressed grapes
repressed screams
of sun shriveled raisins
and their dreams
interrupted
by a manhood deferred
will she ever sober?
or will they keep handing her glasses
overflowing
with the burden of knowing

i never knew
never knew it would haunt me
the ghost of a little girl
in the desolate mansion
of my manhood

i am a man now
and then
i remember
that i have been charged
one million volts of change

will the ghost of that little girl
ever meet my little girl?
she's one now
she must have been three then
maybe four
she's eighteen now
i'm twenty-five now
i must have been twelve then
my mother said
he was in his thirties
and she's not pressing charges
although she's been indicted
and i can't blame her
i can't calm her
i want to calm her
i want to call him names
but only mine seems to fit

"come on let's see if it fits"
two little boys with a magic marker
marked her and it won't come out
"they put it in me"
"no we didn't"
"what are you talking about"
it's not permanent
it will come out when you wash it
damn, maybe it was permanent

i can't forget
and i hope she doesn't remember
maybe magic marked her
lord, i hope he don't pull no dead rabbits outta that hat
what she gonna do then?
and what was Mary's story?
story of a little girl
with a brother
and a couch

she's got a brother and a couch
a sister locked in a bedroom
and a mother on vacation
lord, don't let her fall asleep
her brother's got keys to her dreams
he keeps them on a chain
that now cuffs his wrists together
mummy doesn't believe he did it
but he's left footprints
on the insides of his sister's eyelids
and they've learned to walk without him
and haunt her daily prayers
and if you rub your fingers
ever so softly
on her inner thigh
she'll stop you
having branded your fingertips

with the footprints of her brother
the disbelief of her mother
and her sister
who called her a slut for sleeping

lord, i've known sleeping women
women who've slept for lives at a time
on sunny afternoons
and purple evenings
women who sleep sound
and live silently
some dreams never to be heard of again
i've known sleeping women
and have learned to tiptoe into their aroma
and caress myself
they've taught me how to sleep
having swallowed the moon
sleep till mid afternoon
and yearn for the silence of night
to sleep sound once again
painters of the wind
who know to open the windows
before closing their eyes
finding glory in the palate of their dreams

she had no dreams that night
the windows had been closed

the worlds of her subconscious
suffocated and bled
rivers of unanticipated shivers
and sounds that were not sleep

she was sound asleep
and he came silently

it wasn't the sun in her eyes
nor the noise of children en route to school
she woke to the rays of an ingrown sun
fungused
that stung more than it burned
a saddened school en route to children
who dared to sleep on a couch
exposed to their schizophrenic brother
only to wake with a new personality
one that doesn't trust
as much as it used to
and wears life jackets
to romantic relation ships
can't stand the touch of fingertips
damn, was that marker permanent?
i hope she don't press charges
i hope they don't press
no more grapes into wine
because she might get drunk again
and fall asleep

Rise and Shine
my mother used to say
pulling back the clouds of covers
that warmed our night
but the fleshy shadows
of that moonless night
stored the venom in its fangs
to extinguish the sun
rise and shine
but how can i
when i have crustied cloud configurations
pasted to my thighs
and snow-covered mountains in my memories
they peak into my daily
and structure my moments
they hide in the corners of my smile
and in the shadows of my laughter
they've stuffed my pillows
with overexposed reels
of ABC after-school specials
and the feathers of woodpeckers
that have bore hollows into the ring of time
that now ring my eyes
and have stumped the withered trunk
of who i am

i must re member
my hands have been tied
behind the back of another day
if only i could have them long enough
to dig up my feet
which have been planted
in the soiled sheets of a harvest
that only hate could reap
i keep trying to forget
but i must re member
and gather the scattered continents
of a self once whole
before they plant flags
and boundary my destiny
push down the warted mountains
that blemish this soiled soul
before the valleys of my conscience
get the best of me
i'll need a passport
just to simply reach the rest of me
a vaccination
for a lesser god's bleak history

☘

i rushed home
from life to life
asleep
my dreams waiting
to not be remembered
my days re membered, past

and i yearn
for the strength and courage
to sucker punch moments
so that they may swell
and ripen blackened blue
like sweetest night

∽

i left my change
on the counter
remained the same
and left the store

having stuffed some dreams
under my shirt
along with a few visions

i knew
i wouldn't
get caught

never have
(avoid possession)

i shared my thoughts
with those less fortunate
in exchange for information
on my whereabouts
they pointed me
in three directions
i stood still
and still
i stand

෮

i drew her
like a bath
then sat and soaked
watching the bubbles
disappear
as a ring
around the tub
gave us the age
of trees

༄

she told me
my father
had burned her
in another lifetime

she also told me
that she loved me

೬౨

sometimes i see you
in the bags beneath my father's eyes
and sometimes he sleeps through the night
on the same two pillows that you do

ᕲᕱ

Q: are you going to follow
in your father's footsteps?

A: my father's footsteps
lead to my mother's bed
where i spent much of my childhood

why return where i have already been?

෧෨

our relationship
seemingly
falling apart
at the seams

but our grandmothers
were both seamstresses
for a reason

       ∾

she says i'm not there for her
i picture her walking through a mansion
opening each door expecting to find me
there's an 8x10 photo of me on the left pane
of each window in every room
i am nowhere to be found

she finally descends into the basement
the furnace is humming
the floor is cold, lifeless concrete
there are spiderwebs and dust heaps
an abandoned science project that smells of vinegar
bags of clothes intended for the salvation army

and a milk crate
where sits this very journal
in which i am now writing
it catches her eye
like the sighting of a nest
on an aimless stroll
she picks it up
contemplating her audacity
and finds herself
here on this very page

she feels she is being watched
she looks over her left shoulder
a ladybug sits there
she is now caught between these words
and an animal instinct that informs her of a predator
she realizes that i am there
somewhere

she skims through these words
for hints of my whereabouts

i love you

"so what" she thinks
as she reads on
"where are you when i need you?
this is not a nurturing relationship
we're not here for each other"

then why else are we here?

she closes the book
frustrated
and walks towards the furnace
she slowly opens the door

i am there
lost in a vision
unable to decipher
the fire that burns me
from the page that writes me

杠

she is leaving me
for the sun
she may be disappointed
when she discovers
that we are twins

∞

he sat
beneath
the double sun
a single child
a lonesome kind
a withered hand
a wintered mind
a changing season
where the sun that sets
is reason

☙

still tonight
you expect me to stand as OSIRIS
when i know that the sun is SET

whom can i trust
when even nature conspires against me?

when the sun descends into its darker side
who will gather my severed pieces?

she looked at me and smiled
and said, "what IS IS

now have faith in the way things are"

AUSAR AUSET

૭૭

i thought she was her
and she is
but sometimes she forgets
and i wonder
and wander
ᕲ

i was wrong
if it was the Red Sea
that i parted
then, like Moses
i was leaving Egypt
and enslavement behind me

although it had been
self-same Egypt
that made me proud

but it is now
that same pride
and self
that will mummify
these moments
if i do not
leave Egypt

yes, i am leaving Egypt
to see the world
i may be back
but this time
i will return
with all the stolen properties
of our libraries

i am going to gather
our severed pieces

how surprised i was
to find ISIS in Germany

there is a scarab
on my throat
i cannot lie

she lives in a graffitied tenement
and recognized me from the distance

(a departure from Africentricity)

෦෨

she is the one
who said "fun"
sounded like a word
of German origin
she thought too much
like me
our time together
like summer
(concentration)
camp
emaciated possibilities
lie lifeless
o, this intellect burns

the crematorium below my nose
keeps life above my ears

silence is the star
that i shall wear
to mark my difference
yet we have so much in common
tonight
that the sun
has made light of it
while we contemplate
the weight of it all

it is we that are emaciated
our bodies subject
to our mind's propaganda
forgive the distinction
but intellect fares
moment's genocide
and we should have kissed
hours ago

you hold your breath
when you should hold your tongue
and hold your tongue
when you should hold my hand
and i should delegate
more authority to myself
but i can't help thinking
that you are thinking
thinking
what is she thinking?

၈၀

intellect is like a major city
laden with concrete and metal
advanced modes of transportation
shining buildings and fenced in parks

spirit is the mountains,
forest, wilderness
and vast countryside
that surrounds it

too many people live in the city
struggling day to day
for mere existence

most have forgotten
how to live off the land

they only experience nature
on class trips and short term vacations

for those that live in the country
cities are like amusement parks
with high prices and temporal satisfaction

at the end of the day
they are tired
ready to go home
to relieve their ringing ears

∽

i am empty
in a non-buddhist way
my energies have gone
to the four directions

the river
never returns
to its source

i have always been empty
and i have always been filled

i must re member
i am not the source

i have overfed my ego
it sits slumped
on a couch
of its own making

it is now time
to call on the goddess

must i engender
divinity?

೦౿

yes, the moon is full
on every night
and every night
is every day

it matters not
which part of you
is lit by the sun
i have adjusted my eyes
to the darkness
and black
has never been
more luminous

i am a witness
to your circumference
i no longer need the sun
to see you

even time is phosphorescent
and your crescent shape
is only an illusion

∽

children rummage through
their mother's altars

꩜

the baby has fallen asleep. i am left to the blue lights of my aquarium and the reflective scales of passing fish. what a day has passed. i woke before the sun and stood before the moon. i held her in my arms and warmed her back to sleep. the morn served us sunrays in bed. we sat up slowly and faced the day. it always seems later than it is. the clock re-minds we spirits of our minds. a fish slowly approaches the glass. and we begin to mind the business of the day. i closed my eyes to recount the journey of the night. but the baby was too hungry to wait. i fed her apples and raspberry patience from the jar. she ate it all and played with the spoon, until i tired of the noise and encouraged a new toy. i played with power. until she tired of the noise and encouraged a new toy. we played the guitar. same song as yesterday. this day promises to be . . . this day. this is the day we looked at pictures of children from around the world: all smiling. she returned to Brazil. as if she had my memories. i kept turning to the next page. as if i had an appointment. we never made it past Japan until this evening, when she was growing tired. this is the day that she walked to the Brooklyn Moon, attempting to enter every gateway that she passed. me, attempting to steer her towards our destination, as if we shared a common destiny. a common sense of direction. a common sense of curiosity. impatience killed the dog. and she would wait, squatting, when i tried to steer her.
i've grown tired
i hope to see you tomorrow
and the sun

she always wakes in time for prayer
in time of prayer

morning meditation
is the burial service
of impressions
made the day before

the naming ceremony
of the day

∽

i chased birds today
i sang on a sphere
changing octaves through fear
wedged my voice into the bark of trees
cleared my throat
and my throat clearly soared
amongst those chased birds

chaste words

in the ghetto of my mind
sentiment's tenement
prolific project

12 story complex
but only one landlord
and i'm behind in rent
and they're threatening
to turn off the lights

section 8 asylum
why do i allow such tenants?
they never pay on time
and actions speak louder than . . .

but i have a million ideological mouths to feed
children who play hooky on the roof of my mouth
and every cavity has its squatters

all this
before a single word is said

i am still
but seldom silent

∞

i live
in a beautiful home
with no natural light
෨

i entered her room
to find her in darkness
standing on a chair
reaching towards
an ever rising ceiling

i knew her mother
walked on the floor above
in the room where
my grandfather once hung

now hangs a chandelier
that will never burn
as bright as he

ᦕ

when will i begin
to write about
darkness and silence
again

i have found the time
to complain about
what this room
does not admit:
sunlight
hints of an outside world

but last night
i slept
in the room
that is visited
by the sun every morning
and realized
the amount of noise
it is also visited by

my room is dark and silent
the sun's light will not reach
in this room
you will learn
to let your light so shine . . .

you will sit in darkness
swallowed by silence
until the angel of solitude
ignites your spine

෴

i have pentagrams for hands
and palms that seldom flicker
let me touch the burning embers
of your soul

High John the Conqueror
awaits you
light my coal

seven candles
come Sept ember
we'll be whole

nine moons
before the days
foretold by runes

ᕤ

two autumns
and i have not
changed enough

∽

i don't trust the man
that i am becoming
he seems too much
and seldom is

෨෮

i see men
very little
yet they seem
in all i hear

椶

there is a mouse
in my room
beneath my altar

i cannot see it
but this is no metaphor
i have seen it

i am the cowardly elephant
who runs from the mouse

i am the foolish mouse
who perceives himself
as an elephant

i am
until i perceive
otherwise

෨

i asked for a sign
and she sent a mouse

i stood cowardly
at the door
surrendering
my altar
my bed
my space

i am too scared
to enter
to share
common ground
with such a common rodent

i believe
i know
where you are
but belief
and knowledge
are what led me
to these questions
in the first place

i have caught
a passing glimpse of you
but now you have become
the unseen

you are nothing
to be afraid of
yet i fear
your presence
and what you symbolize

this is a room of symbols
and you have found your place
within

and now
i sit prostrate
before the altar
i sense you are under
having sensed your true presence
you are a true sight to behold

you could fit perfectly
into the palm of my hand
but your presence
fills this entire space
and i am filled
as you are welcome

౪

i drank blood
with my father
to symbolize
a mother's absence

his father drank a wine
that led to the absence
that it once symbolized

hers is the kiss
that turns symbols
into that which they symbolize

ᕲ

this poetry
has become
about beauty
not about truth

the truth would
have more questions

∾

i simply stopped
writing of truth
when my truths
no longer sounded
triumphant

∽

i simply want to be
the love song
dangling from her lips
unfiltered
ever burning at the end
the beginning forever
at her lips
my dreams
on the tip of her tongue

she breathes
clouds of mystery
once mine
smoke signals
another lifetime
now dissolved
into thin air

and when
the mystery is gone
so is the fire

maybe if i came in packs
(like wolves)
but there'd still be the warning
for pregnant women

love's suffering addiction
can turn hearts yellow

i want to be
the one she calls
on her cigarette break
not the cause of it

ᄋᄼᄼ

we sleep
in the same house
but it is we
who have a
long distance relationship

෨

oftimes the distance between us is the Atlantic. and we are sitting right next to each other. i am not certain as to whether one of these thoughts could chart the distance to your heart. regardless, i bundle as many of my emotions as i can: thoughts chained to feelings, malnourished intentions, unspoken dimensions. as living cargo they journey to moon risen sea to your ear. many will not make it. i am shore. rations are minimal. and it is hard to maintain an emotion with minimal rations. transporting passions. middle passage. they are not willing cargo. it is I that will. but this upper-case *I* is rare. maybe it would be simpler to bottle them and see if they reach. but haven't i bottled enough emotion without ever receiving a letter in return? i've been given two weeks notice. that's a fortnight until we know the fate of the sun.

∞

they say
that i am a poet

i wonder what
they would say
if they saw me
from the inside

i bottle
emotions
and place them
into the sea
for others
to unbottle
on distant shores

i am unsure
as to whether
they ever reach
and for that matter
as to whether
i ever get
my point
across

or my love

ೋ

even my pen man ship
throws thoughts overboard
into a black ink sea

and how many thoughts perish
before they reach the page?

∽

i had begun
to point my pen
at her heart

∽

i do not mean
to exploit our relationship

all that i have
learned from you
i cherish most

should i keep it to myself?
should i keep you to myself?

i want to tell my mother
what i have learned

what is personal?
should i code what i say?

i say so little
too much

when meanings are already hidden
should i hide them?

what am i going to keep for myself?

the wild woman is unkempt
the changing woman is unkempt

she speaks her mind
that is a great thing
for a woman

as it is for a man
to speak his heart

he art

do i not serve a purpose?

did i make this up
to give myself
a sense of fulfillment?
is this ego play?

and am i writing this
for an audience?

i do not wish
to lose my mind
only to find my heart

or should i?

she knows what she is talking about
exploitation: to share resources
that are not yours to share

what is mine to give?

excuse me
if i do not speak
in metaphor

may i be forward?

before word
is intent

everything she tells me
i immediately place
in my argument
against her
proving her abusiveness

but is she?
or am i simply
placing her statements
in an abusive paradigm

∞

is it ideas that i love?
well framed thoughts?

there are many galleries
that sit unattended
never communing
with the common

then actions are graffitied ideas

my eyes are closing
as my heart opens
so does this book

　　　∽

i write in red ink
that turns blue
when the book closes
〄

sometimes our thoughts and feelings
are our most prized possessions

and then there are times
to let go of your possessions
and wander

ᕲᕲ

i fear your freedom
thus, i must fear my own
you are a changing woman
i recognize you
and am trying to free you
of me

it is your freedom
that i love
i have not yet
learned to love
without holding on

∽

she held my hand
leaving three fingers
in my grip

like gripping a symbol
from the i ching
which i'm not sure
i've ever grasped

ꙮ

and the thing is
the only reason
why i have difficulty
trusting you
is because i know
how easy it has become
for me to lie

೧୨

i lie to you
about twice a day

૭૭

this hurts

hypocrisy is a strange word
when said
it never exits the mouth
it stays there
on the roof of the mouth
hovering
like a two-headed bird
owl/vulture
both stalking prey
now living
now dead

. . . and the magioian
who leaves judgment
suspended in mid air
his white gloves
chase a hollow truth
to the density
of death
he holds the rabbit
by its ears
and shakes the feces
from his top hat

all while the audience applauds
he turns to his graceful assistant . . .

ଓଓ

here is a picture of me
waiting at the gateway

we had to come
our separate ways

i know you will
arrive on time
for our departure

it is because you traveled
under someone else's name
that this now happens
but that has saved us money
and makes complete sense
since we know
we will meet up
before departure

∽

i have never
flown over a desert
more expansive
than tonight
∽

what am i waiting up for?

love never comes home
until fear, possession, and jealousy
are far gone
sage has burnt
and fresh candles lit
and by that time
i may be asleep

༄

in an attempt
to not lose
a prized possession
i lost everything

∞

i will sleep
to mold a mask of dreams
to wear to tomorrow's festival

no one will recognize me
they will all mistake me
for someone other
than themselves

∽

on the edge
of the bed
she sat

her birth certificate
in her hand
tears in her eyes

she said
i am home sick

our daughter
cradles a doll
in front of the fireplace

ʊᶜᵕ

she is lonely
in my presence
and i understand

i am within
and have not
learned to be
two places at once

have not
learned
to be

i live and walk
but my thoughts
nurture a child
unborn
∽

i once wrote out of loneliness
and into it

please, not now, love
i'm suffering

somebody dipped this soul
in Christian batter
fried it

and then
made the mistake
of trying to serve it back to me

as if
i wouldn't taste my own being
obscured by a confectionery sugar

∾

she says
she responds
to my hugs
like a battered woman
who is offered chocolate
by her batterer

invisible scars
take the longest
to heal

look
don't we make
beautiful victims?

i am wearing
orange wool flat-front slacks
with tear stains above the knee

the white cashmere sweater
is perfect for frowning

don't we hold our ground wonderfully?
will we ever choose to hold the sky?

but then
the sky cannot be held
as the wind cannot be caged

∾

she has taken sides
with the wind

a gust of passion
now gone

she perhaps inspired
my grandest idea
of myself

which i cashed in
before my seventh year

༄

lost for words
i've lost my intent

if there is no manipulation to be done
will anything be said?

so what is this?

another aim at convincing someone
who already loves me to love me?

is it that i want you
to love me more than you love yourself?

i doubt it

i'm fading
whether it be darkness or light
let it consume me

this is so contrived

∽

words no longer made pretty
honesty of a different brand

we must each choose our words
as you have chosen your silences

∾

i began this book
with a self-imposed
deadline

yet, i have begun
writing towards
the circle of life

౦౦

cemeteries
are our only
tended gardens

we tend to die

∽

your kiss
is a shallow grave

i am coming back

෩

to aim
is to take oneself too seriously
by focusing *without* instead of *within*

re arrange and re member

aim . . . i am

the right letters are there
it's the wrong composition

☙

i am a poet
who composes
what the world proses
and proses
what the world composes

Kahlil Gibran

ᘒᘐ

i have faith
in who you are becoming

in who you are

you are the wolf
having run through a stream
to stand on a mountain peak
dripping wet

ꝏ

you are drawing me to you
that is your art

i am drawn

୧୬

i drew a blank
and i think
it may be
the best thing
i've ever drawn

∞

draw closer

∾

i am a canvas
painted over
whether it be by your hand
or mine own

a stroke
of genius
is as debilitating

i now sit
perfectly still
closer to the earth
than i have ever been
our love
the equator

paint me, love

i am a painting
in reverse

my blues
will disappear
as Will . . .
arises

Solstice Will i am

arise, fair love
and face the glorious morn

on this
the shortest day of the year
it has become
too bright
to write

December 21, 1998

∾

epilogue

and they began to cough up the universe's distortion: a yellowish mucus that clogged their nose and chest. they slept and dreamt in startling clarity. awake, they would stare into seemingly blank space. perhaps they could not decipher what they saw. but that is probably not the case. they were sick with understanding, an understanding that practically dripped from their ears. many of them believed they were dying. they sat in their beds refiguring their diets. they thumbed through books adding up their symptoms to determine specific ailments. they created tonics and dug up age old remedies. but it was that which was age old that they were coughing up: balls of tissue heaped like pyramids at the side of a bed. flus go around like wake-up calls. and one by one they woke. their clarity sometimes frightened them. they were not used to this brand of understanding that charged them with the inevitable power of disrupting comfort zones. in a new age, such as this, comfort zones are the first to go. when two or three gathered they would glow. they were attracted to each other like crystal clusters. the very likes of which remain on her fingers. the question remains, like steaming heaps of ruins of newly bombed cities. we wander aimlessly, perhaps, only to find the ring of a loved one, now gone . . . and i pose questions as if there were a camera.

⌒